Originally published as *Co robią uczucia?* by Wydawnictwo Dwie Siostry, Warsaw, 2020.

First Elsewhere Edition, 2022

Library of Congress Cataloging-in-Publication Data available upon request.

Elsewhere Editions
232 Third Street #A111
Brooklyn, NY 11215
www.elsewhereeditions.org

Distributed by Penguin Random House
www.penguinrandomhouse.com

Funding for the translation of this book was provided by a grant from the Carl Lesnor Family Foundation.
This work was made possible by the New York State Council on the Arts with the support of the office of
the Governor of New York and the New York State Legislature. This publication has been supported by the
©POLAND Translation Program. Archipelago Books also gratefully acknowledges the generous support
of Lannan Foundation, Cornelia and Michael Bessie Foundation, Jan Michalski Foundation, the National
Endowment for the Arts, and the New York City Department of Cultural Affairs.

PRINTED IN CHINA

Third Printing

Tina Oziewicz

What Feelings Do When No One's Looking

Illustrated by Aleksandra Zając
Translated from the Polish by Jennifer Croft

elsewhere editions

Curiosity always climbs as high as possible –
to the treetop, the roof, or the chimney.

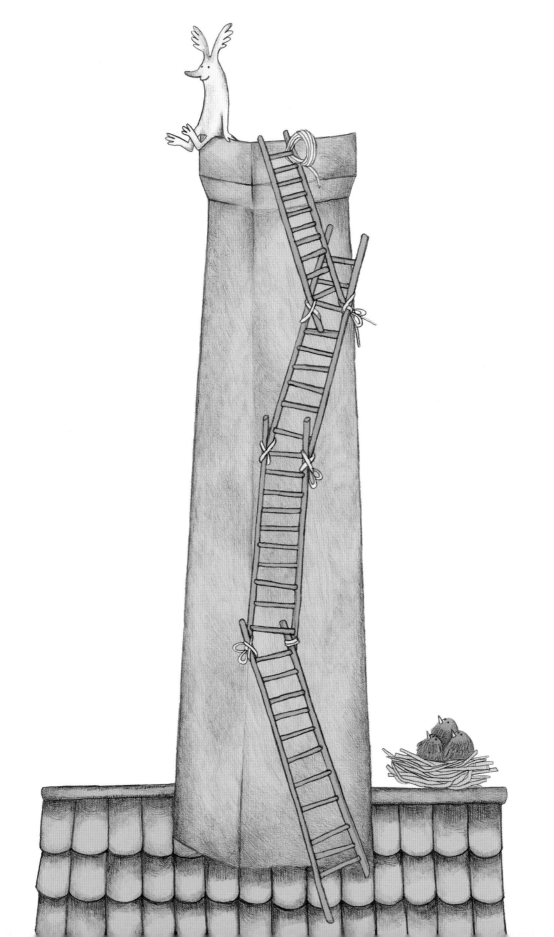

Joy bounces on a trampoline.

Gratitude warms.

Jitters sit in a rusty can in a dark corner under a wardrobe.
That's where they have their favorite hiding place, without a door or windows.
They look out at the world through the tiny sliver under the lid.

Imagination travels an unbeaten path.

Calm pets a dog.

Envy tramples all that is beautiful.
No time to rest – there are so
many beautiful things to ruin!

Insecurities build cages.

Freedom sails.

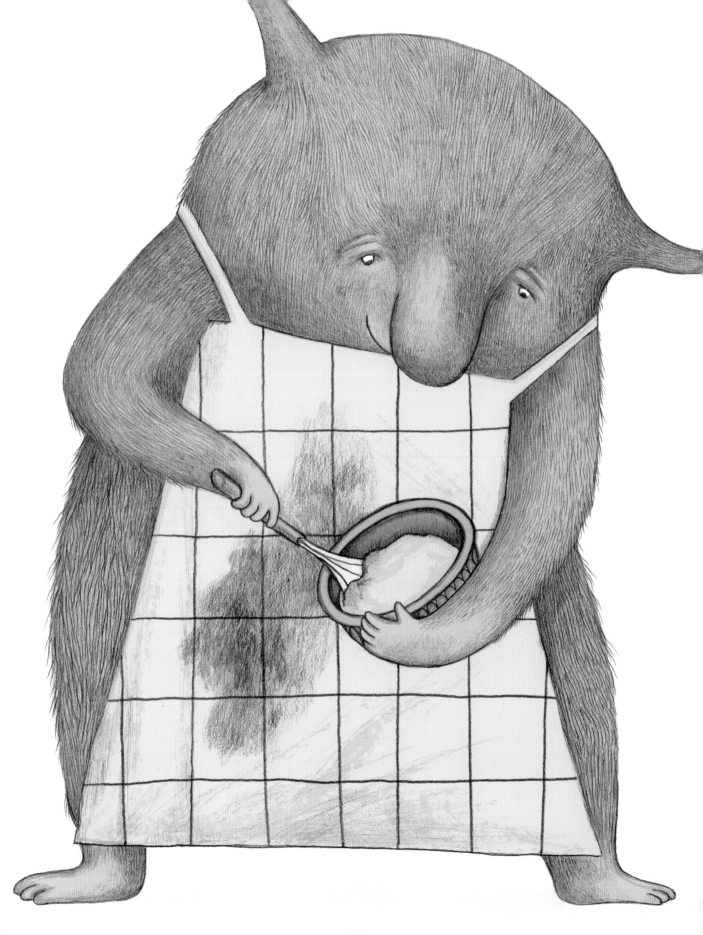

Hospitality bakes a cake.

Compassion helps snails cross sidewalks.

Shame
digs little holes
and burrows inside them
like a mole.

Pride stands tall in a tower at the summit of a crystal mountain.

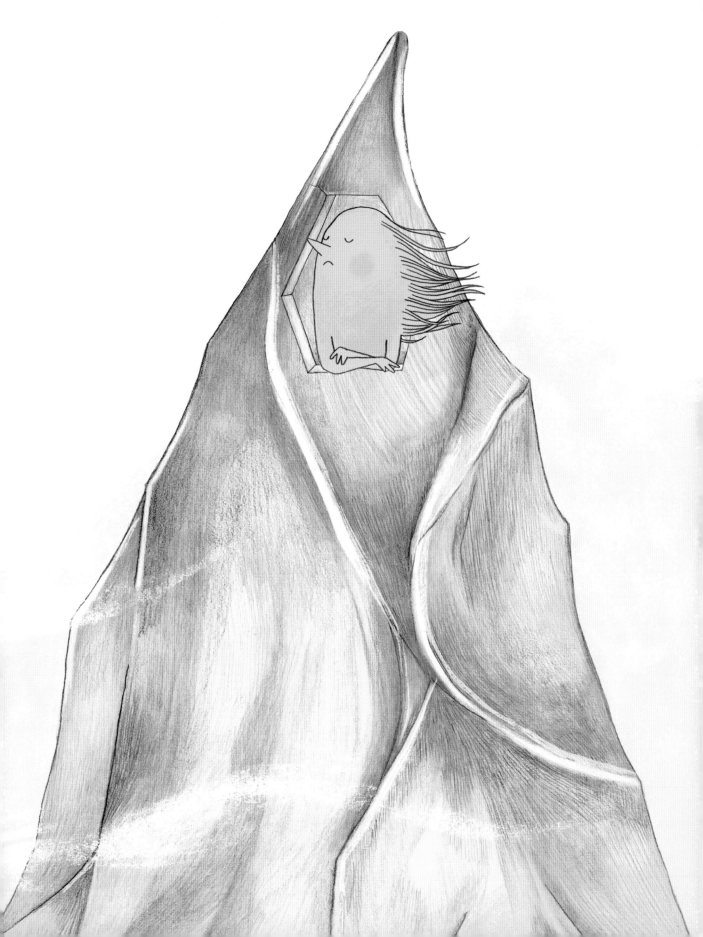

Courage takes a rest in the very heart of the forest.

Happiness zips through the air in a soap bubble.

Patience keeps a lovely garden.

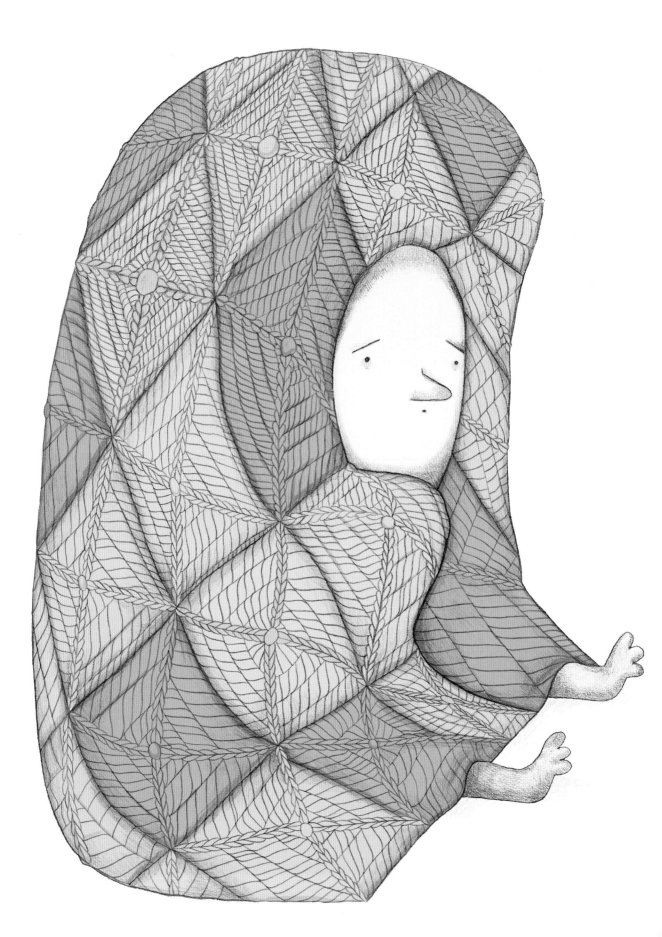

Sadness covers itself up with a blanket.

Trust builds bridges.

Anxiety juggles.

Nostalgia sniffs a scarf.

Kindness quiets the storm.

Excitement races to a friend with a newly discovered book.

Anger explodes.

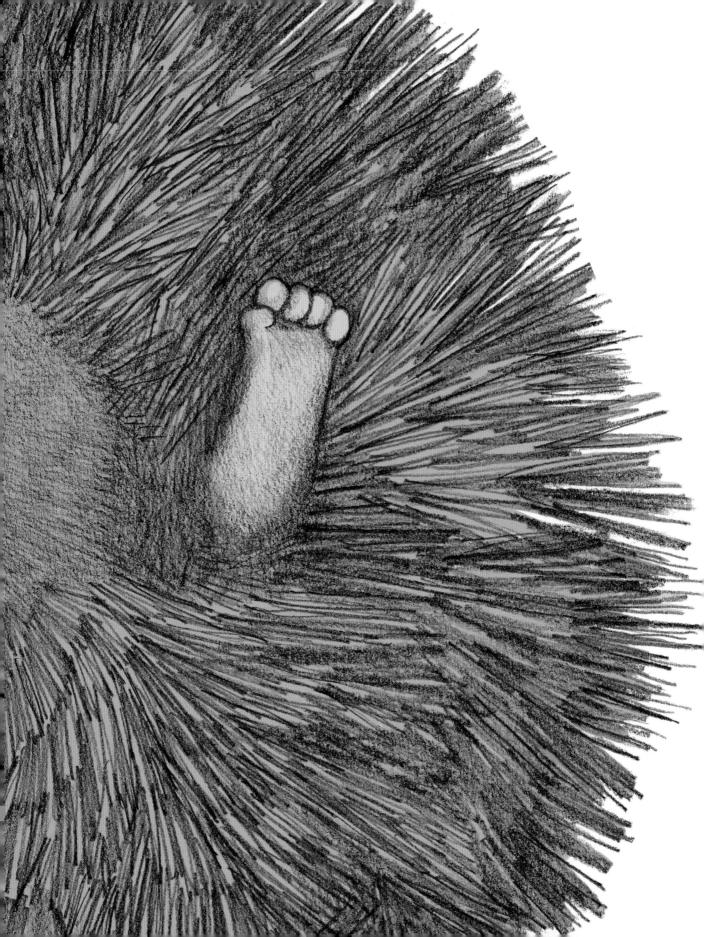

Fear pretends
it isn't there.

Bliss sits in a nice chair
with a cup of tea in its paws.

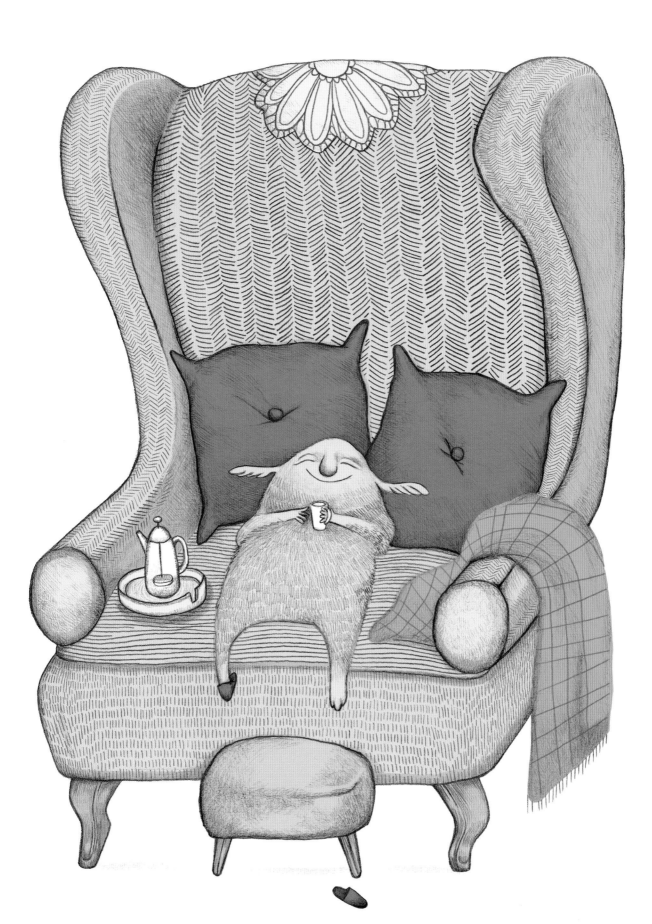

Longing travels.

Hope makes a sandwich for the road.

Loneliness trudges through the desert.

Hate chews through links and cables.
Can't connect!
Can't connect!

Friendship sits down beside you when you trip and fall.

Love is an electrician.

And where does all this live?

In us.